FIVE
PSALMS

Peter McDonald

AGENDA EDITIONS

ISBN 978-1-908527-40-0

First published in 2021 by

Agenda Editions
Harts Cottage,
Stonehurst Lane,
Five Ashes,
Mayfield,
East Sussex
TN20 6LL

Design and production by JAC design
Crowborough, East Sussex TN6 1DH

Printed and bound in Great Britain by
T J Books Ltd, Padstow, Cornwall

Peter McDonald is a Northern Irish poet and critic. He has published seven full-length volumes of poetry, most recently *The Gifts of Fortune* (Carcanet, 2020); his *Collected Poems* (Carcanet) appeared in 2012. As a translator, he has published *The Homeric Hymns* (Fyfield Books/Carcanet, 2016). His literary criticism includes *Serious Poetry: Form and Authority from Yeats to Hill* (OUP, 2002) and *Sound Intentions: The Workings of Rhyme in Nineteenth-Century Poetry* (OUP, 2012). He has edited *Louis MacNeice: Collected Poems* (Faber, 2007) and two volumes of the Longman *Poems of W.B. Yeats* (Routledge, 2020). Since 1999, he has been Christopher Tower Student and Tutor in Poetry in the English Language at Christ Church, Oxford, and is also Professor of British and Irish Poetry in the University of Oxford.

for Martyn Percy

Contents

Psalm 98   7

Paraphrases on *Psalm 98*   9

Psalm 25   13

Paraphrases on *Psalm 25*   17

Psalm 94   21

Paraphrases on *Psalm 94*   24

Psalm 8   29

Paraphrases on *Psalm 8*   32

Psalm 114   35

Paraphrases on *Psalm 114*   37

Psalm 98

1   *Sing out, and when you sing for God the song*
           is always new, as it has to be
    since every thing he does, each single thing
           is made distinct and clear to see:
    his right hand, his arm stretched out, bring
           fresh havens to us, sanctity.

2   *For God has let us see deliverance:*
           he has put his justice in full view
    of the whole world, so in every instance
           it stands revealed and again new.

3   *He has remembered his love and his trust*
           for the family of Israel;
    about our God's salvation, the farthest
           limits of the wide earth can tell.

4   *Split all the air with praises of the Lord;*
           that self-same earth, sing out to him,
    and let the music of your every word
           sound out and then resound through time.

5   *Play on strings of the harp for God; for him*
           let your harp be the call of a psalm.

6   *In the Lord's presence, with trumpet and shofar,*
           again make joy split all the air.

7   *Let the sea roar, let all of the sea roar,*
           the dry land, and those who live there;

8   *let waves slamming in waves be clapping hands,*
           shouts echoing through hilly lands

9   *in the Lord's very presence, when he comes*
           to give the world justice, for then
    he will settle with the people their due sums
           in equal reckoning for all men.

Paraphrases on *Psalm 98*

Not one thing that can take the place
   of another thing: remember that,
   chew/suck on that,
take notice, hold your peace,

chew it like endless bubble-gum,
suck it like a big boiled sweet:

whatever comes from you has to come
   new every time
and new is natural to him,

a billion billion facets of the earth
   new and unrepeatable
in his hand like the works of his hand,
   like grains of sand

but his palm never gets full:
   a place of safety, a space
   without need of alarm
at *death, that dark spirit, in's nervy arm.*

*

My dad would stretch his arm out, palm
the gobstopper I'd just unwrapped:
you could choke on that he snapped,
and it wasn't like him.
Maybe something had happened long ago,
something had happened to someone he knew,
but I never found out. I can see his hand
now: it's both strong and delicate,
the second finger raised, barely inclined
to touch the things held in it.

*

A penny sheet of bubble-gum
pink, with a layer of sweet dust,
was dangerous to swallow.
Now it is bright as new.

I'm watching the sunset over Shandon Park:
    orange and pale reds against the dark
at the edges of the earth. Let trouble come.

*

Band after band, and the noise is
    almost visible in waves
of pain: though I press my ears as

they go past, it's no good, and I whine
    and finally scream
to be taken away, taken home,

away from the skull-splitting music,
    when fifes cut the air like knives,
with the lambegs like some factory machine

slamming its rivets in, and the massed hum
    and wheeze of sickly accordions
as they carry the melody of a hymn.

*

The sea is also the terror of the sea:
the sound the water makes is a dead sound
that comes to life, that you can hear inland,
that is locked somewhere within the mountains even
and waits to emerge, to split rocks and take the ground with it
into a world transfigured to sheer noise
where water judges the dry land without end.

*

Upright women and men
as they would reckon
themselves, and on firm ground

   so the evil done
   is not evil
   or else not done:
   it's all clever, civil

and foul, answering to no one,
assuming there is nobody around
and only the victim can be liable.

There is a layer of dirt in the soul
you can't see, though it can be seen;
none of us goes at our own reckoning:
we shall pay in full; we shall be paid in full.

Psalm 25

1   *I lift, Jehovah, I lift high*
       to you my breathing soul;
2   *I take the shelter you supply*
       that my strength may not fail

     when those who hate me jump for joy,
       Lord God, in victory;
3   *but those who poison and destroy*
       in darkness you will see,

     and take their strength, while you give strength
       to those who wait for you:
4   *show me the paths, Lord, the whole length*
       of the route I travel through.

5   *Walk with me in the truth, and keep*
       me right, God of my peace;
    in patience, as I wake or sleep,
       my waiting does not cease.

6   *Remember, Lord, your care for me,*
       the goodness you once gave,
    that leads back to infinity,
       and is always mine to have.

7   *As for my sins when I was young,*
       do not remember those,
    Lord God, from whom all mercy sprung
       and all goodness arose.

8   *For God is good, and he sets straight*
       wanderers from the road;
9   *he guides the needy, and with great*
       mercy takes up their load.

10   *All of God's ways are truthfulness*
      and kindness towards those
    who keep their binding promises
      to him, keep his laws close.

11   *So by your name, Jehovah, now*
      forgive my wicked deeds,
    their number greater than I know
      where evil swells and breeds.

12   *Who is the man that fears the Lord?*
      As he chooses, God will teach
13   *the way to him; his soul's reward*
      will be that he lives rich

    and passes on to all his sons
      the riches of the earth:
14   *God's secret belongs to the ones*
      who know that secret's worth

    and fear him – for to these he shows
15   *his covenant; always*
    my eyes follow where the Lord goes,
      knowing that he will raise

    my feet from each ensnaring net.
16   *Turn to me, pity me:*
    from every side I am beset,
      and caught in misery.

17   *My heart's troubles are without bound:*
      lead me from sorrow's pass;
18   *see my distress, sin's leaden bond,*
      and lift away its mass;

19   *see those who hate me, for they are*
          many, and growing more,
    while the great hatred that they share
          is violent and sore.

20   *Hedge round my breathing soul, and let*
          me never faint or fail:
    all of my trust in you I put;
          let my cheeks not grow pale.

21   *Let wholeness and let righteousness*
          protect me on the way;
    at every step, in every place,
          it is for you I stay.

22   *Defend, O Lord, save and restore*
          at each turn and travail
    this place and people evermore,
          this very Israel.

Paraphrases on *Psalm 25*

In theory, I was *en route*
from somewhere definite to somewhere else,
but really I was waiting.

                I might have come
from anywhere; I might never go.

                   If the train
drew in now, I could scarcely
hold my head up, or hold myself up
without somebody to lend a hand.

         *

        The road is a dream
in which you can't be lost
though you don't know yet where you are.

The right way is the road in the dream
       and the route found that was lost
          just where you are.

         *

I told myself I couldn't help myself
and went straight on ahead. I knew the road
was twisting round too far, bent out of true,
and all of this was – what was the word for it,
sin? – something more than the heart could take.
The heart, indeed: for fuck's sake, the heart?

         *

Yet I could talk the talk.
At my age, I could be
in a pale suit running
a tabernacle, an out-
of-town warehouse
of poor souls stacked
to the rafters: the Lord
God would walk beside me
on the narrow way, and I'd
nor faint nor fail, my
patience unbreakable
unto death, unto death,
in the faith that sin's
dead weight shall be lifted,
lifted up, lifted away,
in the keeping of his laws.
I could talk, I could spell
out that covenant.

*

You will be loved, and you will be hated.
The first you'll want to believe, too much,
and the second you'll try not to believe,
but both are true. And now the days of your youth
are a fable, hard to read: the road you're on
must have started somewhere, it must be
going somewhere else – but that doesn't help.
This far in, you just can't help yourself.

The feeling is like love when you've lost love:
you don't believe that it was ever real.
Hatred too you have to work to realise –
you can't see them, yet they really want you dead
and are waiting, as you also learn to wait, in
helplessness, fatigue and disbelief, in fear.

*

The floral tribute of a black rose.
A man is caught in a thick net
from underneath; or he searches the sky
for something to kill. A man alone
is lethal. I try to explain
Coleridge's Mariner, and I end up
with Willie Nelson – *the Devil made me
do it the first time; the second time
I done it on my own.* I don't
know where I am, or where I
came from: only what I've done.
As for my heart – shit –
I think my heart has gone.

*

Penn Station thirty years ago:
me waiting, a bad traveller,
for that evening's Amtrak to show,
and not so much as noticing her

until she was standing at my side,
her young black face stricken and sad,
cheeks shiny and puffy where she'd cried
all day with all the strength she had.

But when she spoke, her voice was sure
and true-pitched in its dignity:
*Will you help me, sir? for I swear
I can't help myself.* She could see

me shuffle my feet and look away.
Still broken, she moved on; and when
God searches my face on the last day
it will be her face I see then.

*

The journey, though, is not
        the journey home.
Your cheeks are pale with shame:
        sins of your youth
aren't even the half of it.
        The way of truth
twists from the way of comfort:
        truth is a dark
saying, a score, a mark.

                    *

He is the shelter on the way.
You do not know where the road leads

except one day this breathing soul
is forfeit, and no longer breathes:

its breath is taken in the breath
of all his people on the way

who do not know where the road leads
beyond the shelter of his law.

Psalm 94

1-3   *God of vengeance, Jehovah, God*
of vengeance, the judge of this world,
rise up and dole out to the proud
their punishment: for how long, Lord,
for how long now will
the wicked still prevail?

4-5   *When they open their mouths, they blurt*
out insolence; as soon as they start
to speak, they speak in their own praise,
these schemers of ruin. Lord, it is your
people they shatter when they lay
your legacy waste; the foreigner

6-8   *and the widow they murder, the orphans*
they kill; and then they boast God does
not see them, not notice them once:
they say that the God of Jacob pays
no heed. Beasts of the people, heed
this, if it is sense you need:

9-10   *Does the maker of the ear not hear?*
Does the maker of the eye not see?
The world's great teacher is severe,
so will he not correct you too?
What he offers to men freely
is all there is mankind can know.

11-13   *For the Lord reads the thoughts of men,*
and he sees how people's thoughts are vain.
Lord God, anyone you teach
is blessed, whoever you instruct
in your law, for you give to each
the consolation he can exact

13-15   *from days of evil, patient until*
a deep pit for the wicked is dug.
The Lord will not disown his people
or desert all they inherit:
his judgement will for ever hug
truth close, and the straight heart follows it.

16-18   *Who will stand for me against*
the wicked? Who will stand for me
against wrongdoers? There is only
the Lord: if he had not helped,
then my soul would have been silenced;
and wherever my foot has slipped,

18-20   *your mercy, Lord, holds me secure;*
your comforts give joy to my soul
while within me everywhere
worries jostle. When it does wrong, shall
power that pretends to be the law
ever have you for its fellow?

21-22   *Still they huddle together, bent*
on their benches of authority
to impugn the upright, to see
the ruin of the innocent.
Jehovah has been a defender for me,
and my God the rock of safety:

23   *he has brought down the whole roof*
of their wickedness over them, down
on their own heads, and in
the midst of all their wily plans
he has cut them off: and so again
Jehovah, our God, will cut them off.

Paraphrases on *Psalm 94*

Imagine if the old
diction came to life;
if the measure doled
out by the God of love
to the wicked and the proud
in their high places made
him the God of vengeance;
an extreme and all-at-once
reflex of sheer
rebuke and terror,
unimaginable
in the words' vacancy,
their dereliction;
yet proving to be
real after all,
and the moment of downfall
for the wicked, the proud,
no fiction.

*

The emptier the language, the louder the talk.
The subtler the gesture, the deeper the power.
The more rigged the game, the higher the stake.
The darker the soul, the brighter the PR.

*

To be so old
that you believe in the consequences of words,
            to be so old
that you believe in the reality of wickedness,
            to be so old
that you can remember when pride was a sin;
not to be so innocent about any of this
            that you can be bought and sold.

*

We can game this one; we can play them.
As long as we sound reasonable, anything goes.
The whole point is to mean the lies we choose.
And use his first name when you destroy him.

*

Rilke heard a tree
growing in the ear:
it was a going over
and above, perpetually.

God planted the ear
like a tree,
so what he can hear
is the poetry

of all that's there:
badness, noise,
and good held in poise
precariously.

*

The proud have ears only for themselves;
their sharp eyes are eyes trained in the mirror;
God sees their every image as it dissolves;
he hears the words they don't believe he will hear.

*

As the rain came on, I was stuck
on a muddy overhang the boys
said was easy, and now the noise
from below me was them in a ruck

laughing their heads off: when I grabbed
at a bared root, it just about took
my weight, and although my hands shook
and wet soil gave where brambles stabbed,

I hauled myself crying up to the edge.
They had set me on that stupid climb
for badness: they whooped every time
my foot slipped on a crumbling ledge.

I said nothing. It felt like shame
as I walked home alone, wet through.
For all that, the silence was true:
I listened in it for a name.

                    *

They may be laughing now, but they're not joking:
they've paid the lawyers to make them come out clean;
they write how they want you drowned in the lock, broken,
but heaven help you if you say that's what they mean.

                    *

Words are real; meanings are real; words
really have meanings. You are so old
you can remember how you used to be told
routinely this kind of attitude towards
'discourse' would surely mark you out as stupid
in the company of intellectuals: they
seemed harmless, but behind all that display
of brainy *chic* the pride was turning putrid,

and now high places they saw themselves in
belong to them, while your place is just rented:
take yourself off; get out; don't make them
fight you, for they can afford to win,
and if the words are wrong, they can fake them.
They said they wanted you dead as if they meant it.

*

I say the words, and know they are not empty:
wrongdoers, evil, wickedness; for God
has dug a deep pit to receive those weights.
The roof will come down on their own heads,
even while they're laughing their heads off.

Other words also are real; I will start
to say them over, so they grow in time
inside the ear, to make a psalm:
God's law, the blessed, the innocent,
the upright, the patient, the straight of heart.

Psalm 8

1   *Jehovah, ruler of us, how strong*
     your name is over all the earth,
     you who have blazed your light along
     the night-and day-skies, and all beneath.

2   *In the breath of the unweaned, the breath*
     of babies sucking at the breast
     you put the strength to defy death
     and once and for all set to rest
     the workings and fierce jealousies
     of the last of your enemies.

3   *I look, and I see everywhere*
     your handiwork through all those skies:
     the moon, star glittering against star
     that with your fingers you made rise.

4   *Beneath these, what is a mortal man*
     for you to notice him? And what
     are his descendants, that you can
     still reckon them with eyes not shut?

5   *Yet you made man a little less*
     than the deathless angels in your sight,
     giving him worth in heaviness
     and an impalpable crown of light;

6   *over your hands' work dominion,*
     and over the earth he walks upon;

7   *over the ambling flocks of sheep,*
     and herds of cattle on the move;
     over all the dumb beasts that keep
     together in each field and grove;

8   *over the small birds in the skies*
    and scattering fish that cross the sea
    on high roads many times their size
    through water's brash cacophony.

9   *Jehovah, ruler of us, how strong*
    your name is over all the earth.

Paraphrases on *Psalm 8*

Jehovah is not Jove, for Jove
is only a name; and Jehovah is
in the saying of the name, in the breath
taken to say it – the power of an arm,
a power that pulses and extends
over us all to light the skies
through shadows in the daytime, stars at night.

*

A baby at the breast
turns tiny breaths to strength,
sucking away at rest,
charging its whole length
with what will make it strong,
and feeding there so long
time becomes measureless:
no syllable of address
in that small pulse of sound
as the head begins to nod,
but there, then all around,
the very name of God.

*

There is a silence that reduces to silence
everything loud, all voices that burst
with fury, with pain, with deep hate,

that sends them scattering
like fish, like a shoal of pins
catching light in the water as they dive.

*

The moon and the stars. The moon and the stars.
I imagine them made twice over, made
over a thousand times, a million, more,
and steady everywhere at your fingers' ends.

*

A sky of daylight, then a sky of stars,
but there are no ladders, there are no stairs

between me and that multitude of lights
assembling like angels on the heights:

the first time I properly looked at them
I was nine, and in the planetarium.

*

You'd think if you cried enough somebody would notice,
            but that's not a given;
and that your brilliance, all your glorious achievements,
            would dazzle heaven:

it isn't so, and heaven is where it was always,
            over and above,
yet maybe watching, though with no kind of attention
            that you could prove,

somehow perhaps allowing you whatever influence
            over things you have,
your strength on the earth, the power of your arm stretching
            this side of the grave.

*

The road there was through orchards
and before that through farms,
the sheep and the slow cattle,
all beasts of the field
moving for us, reluctantly:
everywhere, boughs were bending down
low with their weight of fruit.

*

On the bus home, I closed my eyes
        to see those stars, the size

of pinheads in the dark of space:
        behind my human face

their lights caught up in the skies' dish
        turned into tiny fish

and scattered on their different roads,
        so many weightless loads

in the traffic noise that I took to be
        the cold noise of the sea.

*

All of the sounds are one sound in the end
that can't be named, that is its own name,
and reaches into everything there is
like an arm, or like a hand on an arm;
like a hand, or like the fingers on a hand.

Psalm 114

1   *When Israel as a people walked*
away from Egypt, and the house
of Jacob left a place that talked

a foreign language, then it was
2   *Judah became their sanctuary*
and the land the land of Israel

3   *to possess; it was then the sea*
departed, witnessing it all,
and then that Jordan was pushed back:

4   *like rams the mountains reared and danced,*
and like lambs the low hills pranced.
5   *Ocean, what made you run away?*

Why did you, Jordan, change your track,
6   *and you mountains that jumped like rams,*
you lower hills, that skipped like lambs?

7   *Tremble, earth, for the Lord is here:*
quake in the face of Jacob's God
8   *who has turned the rocks where they stood*

to watered fields, and who has made
from flint a fountain where the pure
waters perpetually pour.

Paraphrases on *Psalm 114*

For weeks on end, it was hotter
inside than out: that was the way.

The land was enormous, and not yours;
one day was much like another day.

There was nothing to be done, until
it was done, and nothing to say:

you could talk to them, they gave you jobs
to do; you weren't obliged to obey.

But their very tongue was a prison
whose every word would make you stay

when really there was no point in talking.
Sometimes you have to walk away.

*

What little land there is
                    that I can call my own
has just a house on it
                    and a scrap of weedy garden;
the land of my sanctuary
                    is not much more than a beach,
long and empty, some
                    cliffs and a mile or two
of cliff-walks, a stretch
                    of sky across the sea;
rock-pools with peculiar
                    small fish, and flora
not seen elsewhere, the tiny
                    clenched blooms of white
and red, sudden lavish
                    toadstools that open up

polka-dot canopies, while in
                    some protected ground
the actual toads are boggling
                    at extinction's edge.
My people are no more than
                    a family, and I walk them
into this nameless land
                    I name the land of refuge.

*

The light was blue and pale green, beating
as waves pushed up to and over
bare chalk, that from the cave was
an oval window on the sea.

Standing there, you felt after a while
it must have been the rocks moving
upwards away, and the sea falling
that you watched from that damp tunnel.

Above, the path led to a border
you couldn't cross, and the midday
sun flashed on signs to Rosh Hanikra,
the inland and coast-roads of Israel.

*

If you only see time from where you are in it
then solid ground, like the hills and the mountains,
never moves; but time is not just where you are,
and the rocks and all the waters of the world
change places, dance around each other, jump
into and out of patterns, endlessly: they
seem slow only because you're going so fast
over the earth that you can barely register.

Rivers draw back and change their courses, vast
mountain ranges, stacked up and up and up
where nobody sets foot, and the walkable
low hills, their sides covered in livestock,
leap together with the directionless energy
of lambs in the springtime in an open field.

*

Is it as if
everything that
is where it is

was pushed there,
pushed, as
I can feel

the force of what's
gone, what's to
come pushing me?

*

And sometimes, yes, you have to walk.
As I'm standing here, I must block

sunshine as it flattens the air,
but going on my way I clear

more space: there is a shadow still
distinct from me for a short while,

yet as I grow smaller the ground
is land that clouds and sun have gained,

brighter and further, until all
you see is one glow of detail,

bearing that last speck of me late
away. Now I am only light.

*

The house of Jacob and the God of Jacob:
not words in air, but a promise.

A puddle of fresh water on the rock:
not rain, but a miracle.

The way people are drawn to fountains:
not air, but water held in the air.

Summer, 2020